AUBREY BEARDSLEY

Aubrey Beardsley

By
Brian
Reade

Vic-
toria
& Albert
Museum

LONDON: HER MAJESTY'S STATIONERY OFFICE 1966

Large Picture Book No. 32

© *Crown copyright 1966*

First published on the occasion of the Aubrey Beardsley
Exhibition held at the Victoria and Albert Museum
May-September 1966

"The Fra Angelico of Satanism" was what Roger Fry called Aubrey Beardsley. With more relevance we might call him The Master of the Line Block. For that was a role he can always be said to have filled; whereas the approach to subjects like Satanism and Evil has changed beyond recall from a point at which Beardsley's name was uttered with misgiving.

The photo-mechanical method of reproducing prints or drawings by line-blocks was started in the 1870s, and by the 1880s it was established as the cheapest and the easiest method of facsimile reproduction. Though not all of Beardsley's work was reproduced by this method, his drawings, in the majority of cases, were done with the method in mind, and his style of black-and-white art was evolved by making the most of the limitations put upon any draughtsman who wished to get the best effects, that is to say the clearest, the most telling, the most dramatic effects, from the process as it was used then.

Briefly it was, and still is, a process which excludes intermediate tones: it reproduces lines and areas of the same tone value, but nothing in between, no other "colours". The intermediate tones can be suggested only by dots of some sort, or by thinner lines laid close together. Some of the designs in the present book are reproductions by this

I

method of earlier line-blocks from Beardsley's drawings (e.g. Plates 4 and 5). Others are plates made by another and a dearer photo-mechanical method called half-tone, whereby the texture of the fac-simile is broken down into minute black or white dots, so that the intermediate tones can be included. The half-tone process has been used wherever Beardsley's original drawings are reproduced (except in Plate 13) in order to show something of the quality of his draughts-manship which was lost in the line-block method.

This quality combined strength and frailty in an unusual degree. If Beardsley was not one of the most spontaneous, he was certainly one of the most original, of draughtsmen—a strange young man who exter-nalised his strangeness in an art so uncompromising that people of all ages and of all countries were spellbound, even though sometimes repelled, by it.

His work varied, naturally enough, like Blake's. Both artists could produce feeble drawings, and Beardsley's output in a very short life was so large it would be surprising if some of his designs were not derivations of others by him, though all he did was stamped very firmly with his peculiar style. His emotional range was narrow but concentrated, and he gave it full scope in his art. He gave it full scope, that is, despite two powerfully hostile forces: Victorian prudery, which was the negative side of an idealism in other ways admirable; and his own health or lack of health, the physical manifestation of a destructive energy in him which the Victorians called evil. Then he suffered from that scourge of the nineteenth century, tuberculosis, inherited from his grandfather and his father. There were not many artists, or people of any kind, who produced so much, and died so young. Beardsley died when he was twenty-five.

He was born about a year after his sister Mabel in Brighton in 1872, on 21st August. On his father's side his forbears had been London jewellers: his mother's father was an army surgeon named Pitt. But his father was never brought up to any profession or trade and found it difficult to have or to hold an employment. His mother therefore turned to the inevitable occupation of impoverished ladies in those days and became a governess in London, teaching French and the piano. As might have been expected, her son became a precocious connoisseur both of French literature and music, especially as his mother and sister meant more to him than his father, who gradually faded into the background. Among his very earliest surviving drawings are dinner cards and menus made for his mother's friends; and their rewards for these childish efforts went to help the family budget. He was sent first to a prep-school at Hurstpierpoint, and then to another at Epsom, and when free he and his sister would appear occasionally in the drawing-rooms of rich patrons, playing the piano or singing or reciting. In the winter of 1884 he was sent to Brighton Grammar School, where he became a boarder the following year.

It says much for Brighton Grammar School that he prospered in the place, although he took very little notice of anything he was taught. Two intelligent masters, H. A. Payne, his form master at one period, and Arthur William King, his house master, encouraged him to the top of his bent, in drawing, in acting, in writing, in reading and in expanding himself by all sorts of unorthodox means. But he was already a potential invalid. Tuberculosis had been diagnosed in 1879, and for the remainder of his life he went in constant fear that it would increase.

In 1888 he left school with a strong belief in his own significance—yet uncertain in what form that significance should be expressed. His living had to be earned, and all he could do for a time was to accept a post as clerk in a surveyor's office. After a while he found better employment as a clerk in the Guardian Life Insurance Company. But this was equally boring for an odd young man like Beardsley.

His passion for amateur theatricals continued. Even after they had left school his sister and he used to give performances of charades and little comedies at his parents' house in London, all done with high spirits and considerable attention to detail. If he had been strong enough he might have been an actor: his sister indeed became a professional actress. He might even be said to have understood the world as a stage, with himself beside it; yet what was reflected in his art was not the routine of everyday life with intermediate tones, it was a world of ghosts, of condensations from his own preoccupations and memories and desires, often in the surroundings and clothes of some other period. His favoured subjects at first were monsters in what was considered then questionable taste: hermaphrodites and gamine-like women, creatures with the heads of foetuses inspired by medical diagrams, or with the legs of satyrs inspired by similar freaks in Mantegna's engravings. Later on he preferred as fantasies persons who seemed to be subtly abused by life, pierrots and dandies looking infantile or dazed or prematurely old; girls creased by spite or guilt; elderly women corrupted by egotism. In some respects he was an amateur St Anthony.

The jump from being a clerk in an insurance firm to being the widely acclaimed author of this curious world of the imagination took less time than any other development in the history of art. By 1890 Beardsley began to see that drawing was the gift he might best exploit. In the next year he contrived to show some of his untutored efforts to Burne-Jones, who pronounced them full of promise. That decided him; and he spent his evenings making drawings in the Burne-Jones manner or in attending night classes at the Westminster School of Art; while in his lunch hours he would go to Queen Street near the Guardian offices and browse in a bookshop, with the proprietor of which, Frederick Evans, he soon made friends. Evans would exchange books for drawings by Beardsley, and some of these drawings were placed by him in the bookshop window. One day in the autumn of 1892 John Dent, the publisher, was in the shop explaining to Evans how he needed an illustrator for a re-publication of Sir Thomas Malory's *Le Morte d'Arthur*. This was to have plates and decorations printed from line-blocks and not from hand-engraved wood blocks like those used by William Morris at the Kelmscott Press. In other words, it was to be a cheaper production with a wider distribution than any Kelmscott book.

At that moment Beardsley walked into the shop, and Evans introduced him to Dent, recommending him as the artist for Malory. He was provisionally accepted. And after being sent a specimen illustration by him of one of the themes in *Le Morte d'Arthur*, Dent commissioned him to design a graphic framework for the whole of this long legend, with double- and single-page pictures, chapter-headings, ornaments, borders and initials—an undertaking which took Beardsley eighteen months and in the end bored him immensely.

All the same, quite a number of the *Morte d'Arthur* designs were good, though many were wide of the text (e.g. Plates 1–5). Most of them showed traces of the Burne-Jones style deliberately marred, so to speak, by uncanny thoughts; and since he was learning as he went along with this towering job, his designs often reflected features in the works of other artists he admired at the time. He seems to have adapted figures, forms and compositional ideas from paintings by Botticelli, Crivelli and Pollaiuolo which he saw in the National Gallery, and from prints by Dürer and Mantegna which he saw mainly in reproduction. Moreover, he was deeply attracted by Whistler, as a sort of human wasp, and as an artist. The craft of achieving asymmetrical balance in two dimensions as shown in those Japanese prints and fans so fashionable during the Aesthetic period appealed to him also, and this Japanese note was struck with dissonant effects in some of the *Morte d'Arthur* designs, against a medievalism in the Burne-Jones manner (Plate 5). To chords like these were added further notes, notes of grotesque humour, of an odd vein of fantasy, the vehicles of which were the kind of freak that has been mentioned above. Two of the full-page illustrations had to be reproduced in photogravure, they were so complicated, and in one of them dated 8th March, 1893 (Plate 3), Beardsley introduced hair-line details in nightmare profusion, including his own initials, the treble clef sign, a phallus, a spider's web and various types of calligraphic flourish.

Perhaps the most amusing drawings Beardsley ever made were more than a hundred he drew for Dent's *Bon-Mots* series, alongside the bigger commission for the Malory book. These were done mostly in his hairline style, and since he was supposed to be illustrating humorous quips there was no excuse, he felt, not to be witty. But here again the wit was of an extraordinary nature. The small vignettes in the *Bon-Mots* volumes have nothing to do with the texts; many were conceived in the style of the old writing masters of the seventeenth century with pen-line grotesques. Still more were frankly anomalous monsters. The lightness of touch in some of these drawings was due to his growing interest in the French art of his time (Plates 6–10).

If Beardsley was haunted by tuberculosis and constantly weakened by its assaults upon him, at least he had more luck at the beginning of his career than most artists ever dreamt of. No sooner had he been

5

taken up by Dent than he met at a party a man who was about to begin editing a new art magazine, the first number of which was being planned for the spring of 1893. This man was Lewis Hind and the magazine was *The Studio*. Hind was so impressed by some drawings Beardsley showed him on this occasion that he arranged for a selection from them to be reproduced in the first number of *The Studio* to go with an article on the artist by Whistler's friend, Joseph Pennell. On the strength of the article Beardsley became well known to the art world by the middle of 1893, and this led, as soon as could be, to his most famous commission, for the illustrations to Oscar Wilde's *Salomé*, published in 1894.

He had met Wilde in 1891 at the house of Burne-Jones; now he was to see more of him. It has been said that he hated the Lord of Language: the truth is rather he grew to dislike him, having begun by admiring him in the same way that he admired Whistler, as a rare animal, with a remarkable mind. For a time he kept a photograph of Oscar displayed prominently over the fireplace at home, while his attempt to transfer the atmosphere of *Salomé* to his own peculiar art was undertaken sincerely at first. This sincerity took the form of mischief, however, which he may have thought Wilde of all people would enjoy. Certain drawings for *Salomé* had to be turned down because of erotic details, and it must be admitted that some of the series as finally printed include more details of this sort than were ever seen before in an openly published book in England.

The illustrations have lost the force of their pristine impact, having been reproduced and imitated so many times since. But anyone familiar with what was being done in the field of the graphic arts in 1894 can imagine the power of that impact in the 'Nineties. In the first place the drawings evaded the logic of descriptive representation as understood by the Victorians, there being in some of them no backgrounds, and in others background-lines running through images in the foreground (Plate 15). In them Beardsley leaned heavily on motifs adapted from the Peacock Room decorated by Whistler in 1878 (Plate 17). Also the Pre-Raphaelite element was still present but distressed (and this was its magnetic attraction) by an overall grotesque treatment, and by the use of black areas to dramatise the designs after the manner of Japanese print-makers. His unique way of embodying Pater's, and Bacon's, maxims on the beauty of strangeness, the style of certain of his slow-moving lines and rigidly conventionalised trees and roses and peacock feathers, the manner in which he gave decoration and substance equal weight, all became set in the repertory of *art-nouveau* from Glasgow to Milan, and from Germany to the United States; while the short cuts taken by Beardsley, his occasionally near-abstract forms (Plate 18), his concentration on what was essential to the dramatic presentation of the subject—which seemed to be cantilevered on to the page without any of the old and erudite supports—were liberating forces in the development of *avant-garde* artists like Kandinsky and Klee, and even Picasso within the next dozen years.*

In the *Salomé* illustrations Wilde was caricatured several times—conspicuously as a magician, and as The Woman in the Moon (Plate 16); but since Beardsley's caricatures of Whistler as a faun (see cover) and Max Beerbohm as a foetus were being published about then he probably meant, as the saying is, no harm. Whether Wilde objected to the caricatures more than to the eroticism it would be hard to determine. He was clearly irritated by the illustrations, and his instinct was right: they brought fame and ill-fame to Beardsley and helped without doubt to mislead the public into associating Wilde himself with lubricity.

Relations between the two men gradually loosened. Beardsley had become somewhat affected, which may have provoked Wilde to patronise him as though he were still a clever schoolboy. His offered translation of *Salomé* (originally written in French) was rejected by Wilde in favour of another one by Lord Alfred Douglas, and Beardsley interpreted this as a rebuff. Later in 1894, when Beardsley, Henry Harland and John Lane, senior partner in the Bodley Head publishing firm, launched a quarterly periodical, *The Yellow Book*, with Beardsley as art editor, Wilde was annoyed because he was not asked to contribute.

Throughout the years 1893 and 1894 Beardsley received many

* The links between Beardsley and certain twentieth-century artists were revealed in a lecture on Beardsley given by Sir Kenneth Clark at Aldeburgh on 18th June, and again, at the Victoria and Albert Museum, on 18th November, 1965.

commissions for title-pages and frontispieces, published mostly at The Bodley Head (e.g. Plate 19). The appearance of the first number of *The Yellow Book* in April, 1894, brought his name before the general reading public; but the unprecedented style of the drawings by him reproduced in it, the grotesque portrait of Mrs Patrick Campbell the actress, his treatment of the theme of Flaubert's novel *L'Éducation Sentimentale* (Plate 20), a macabre book-plate design and the demi-mondaine *Night Piece* (Plate 21) and cover, all bewildered or disgusted the critics and appealed only to the enlightened among observers. Similar reactions were displayed each time one of the succeeding three numbers of *The Yellow Book* was published. Beardsley had become notorious.

During 1894 he was at the height of such worldly success as he was to enjoy. It was during this period that his work reflected something of London life (e.g. Plates 24–29). His black-and-white conceptions of erotic, mischievous-looking females in exaggerated versions of the clothes of the 'Nineties merged for a time with the aspirations of the New Woman of the period into a mythical entity called The Beardsley Woman (e.g. Plate 29), and caricatures of this personage appeared in *Punch* and other illustrated journals. The rather slangy and painfully haggard young man with his staccato wit was even introduced, though not widely, to the conventional society of dilettanti and clubmen and their wives and daughters. He mixed more with the *fin-de-siècle* writers and artists, who were jealous of him sometimes but comprehended him better. Working mainly at night, nevertheless he enjoyed theatres and concerts and the Wagner operas, and was to be found wherever the game of Decadence was played, at the Café Royal, or at the St. James's Restaurant in Piccadilly, or at the less specialised Thursday evenings of the Pennells in Buckingham Street. Warming himself in this more appreciative atmosphere Beardsley mellowed and shed much of his earlier affectation. In 1894 his style changed again slightly, as a result of his study of Greek vase-painting in the British Museum. The distracting and decorative elements began to disappear, his linear craft acquired forceful clarity and his figures began to be drawn with less emphasis on the grotesque (Plate 32).

In April, 1895, Wilde was arrested after the failure of his libel case against Lord Queensberry, and feeling against him was stirred up by the popular press long before his conviction. He and Beardsley were linked together in the public mind. While an angry mob smashed the windows of the Bodley Head premises in Vigo Street, the headquarters of *The Yellow Book* (to which Wilde never contributed), three Bodley Head authors conspired to put pressure on Lane to sack Beardsley from his post as art editor and to withdraw all designs by him from the next number of the magazine.

Beardsley was left thus suddenly without any means of livelihood. The roomy house in Pimlico where he and his family had lived since 1893 was given up, and thenceforward he existed in a makeshift way. Worse, he felt deeply shocked at the surrounding hostility. From his childhood onwards he seems to have been closely involved with his sister, and it is probable that he was both healed and unbalanced by a mental erethism embracing most forms of deviation, some of which gained physical expression perhaps. Now it appears he sought to demonstrate by heterosexual associations that he was not to be linked with Wilde. The result might have been foreseen: his consumption grew apace and his constitution weakened still more. In this state of decline he was approached by Leonard Smithers, a lawyer turned publisher and bookseller, and much engaged in the commerce of erotica.

It is hard to do justice to Smithers: he was intelligent and gross and knavish and generous by turns. He and Arthur Symons, the writer, founded a new magazine *The Savoy*, with more limited sale than *The Yellow Book*, and in this some of Beardsley's best designs were published during 1896 (Plates 33, 34, 39, 40), together with part of his erotic novel *Venus and Tannhäuser* which came out in *The Savoy* as *Under the Hill*. It was Smithers who published Beardsley's illustrations to *Lysistrata* (e.g. Plate 36), to *The Rape of the Lock* (e.g. Plates 37, 38) and to Ernest Dowson's playlet *The Pierrot of the Minute* (e.g. Plate 41). In the *Lysistrata* drawings Beardsley kept to bold forms without backgrounds and to the skilful arrangement of outlines and dots. The other two series show the influences of Watteau and the illustrators of the *ancien régime* very strongly. In certain passages of *The Rape* illustrations, or embroiderings as Beardsley called them, he suggested intermediate tones in a fully pictorial treatment of his subjects, by the use of dots in gradation unconsciously imitating stipple engraving, or perhaps even the mechanical cells of half-tone reproduction.

It was Smithers too who supported the young artist financially, if unevenly, during these years—at least he thought he did. In fact, by 1896 Beardsley was receiving gratuitous financial support from a platonic admirer Mark André Raffalovich, the rich son of a Russian-Jewish banker; a man-of-letters and a close friend of the poet John Gray; a homosexual who was fired with the ambition to convert Beardsley to Roman Catholicism.

In 1897 Beardsley's art went into a new phase. He produced six illustrations to Gautier's *Mademoiselle de Maupin*, consisting of a frontispiece in water-colour, and five other drawings in indian ink and wash, including The Lady at the Dressing Table (Plate 46), with its echoes of the eighteenth-century painter Longhi, and The Lady with the Monkey (Plate 47). These careful, polished designs in a full scale of tones were published in photogravure by Smithers after Beardsley's death in 1898.

During those years 1896 and 1897, throughout alternating periods of illness and industry in Brussels, in Bournemouth, in Dieppe, in Paris and finally in Menton, Beardsley, like his sister years before, turned to Roman Catholicism, being converted to that faith on 31st March, 1897, at Bournemouth. This was achieved mostly by means of a correspondence between him and his mentor of which only his part survives. If one of the problems of living is the problem of dying, then the aim of Raffalovich was accomplished. Beardsley's last few months, punctuated by the coughing and choking and haemorrhages mentioned so lightly in his letters have in retrospect the phased excruciation of the final scene in *La Bohème*. What he wanted in his twenty-sixth year no doubt was to live, not the artificial respirations of the Church, not the dependence on Raffalovich, not the further dependence on his mother who acted as his nurse. The agonised struggle to be freed from these kindly talons that closed in upon him is suggested by his last work, the illustrations to *Volpone*, Ben Jonson's horrible play, for which he drew inspiration from engravings in seventeenth-century books (e.g. Plates 48, 49); while a similar conflict is suggested by the piety of the letters he sent to Raffalovich and the cynicism of others he wrote to Leonard

Smithers.* The tension broke finally with his despairing note to Smithers, so often published, imploring this dubious person to destroy all his indecent drawings. Nine days after that, on 16th March, 1898, he was dead in Menton. Was this a victory for the Church? Or was it after all a premature victory for Death? It is difficult to be certain. Any attempt to see past the legendary nettles and discreet dock-leaves covering his memory after so many years is likely to be inconclusive.

Beardsley's draughtsmanship consisted of disciplined ink lines over exploratory scribbles (Plate 50): it seldom gave signs of nervous spontaneity. This argues great strength of will as well as great strength of feeling, two vital flames in him that burnt away his declining health. At the same time they were the compensations for an inherited physical handicap. With his almost Neo-Classic coolness he belongs to the winter, not to other seasons of art: he belongs with the artists of night, not with the artists of day. And if some of his work invites brilliant responses it does so through the medium of a levity that was really a sense of loss, transmuted in a dying fire.

According to its rights the established society of his time, with its anthropocentric viewpoint and dwindling reliance on the metaphors of Christian faith, regarded him as unwholesome; while the poets and thinkers of that epoch, and since, thought of him with guilt as Satanic. But with Satanism and the occult he had nothing to do, being too intellectual. Marillier and others have decently insisted he was a satirist, though that would seem to parody Truth by producing from the bottom of her well a set of false teeth. "If I am not grotesque I am nothing," Beardsley said of himself, and in a historical context he can best be appraised as an ironist, neither more nor less, of those last years of the Victorian Age. His flippancy of tone was one expression of that irony: his advance into a mock eighteenth-century dream and into other dream periods was another expression of it. His subjects were often frivolous, yet they need never be taken at face value, and the fact

* I am indebted to Mr Henry Maas for allowing me to see transcripts of the full texts of these letters which he is preparing for publication. The first series was published in mutilated form by John Gray in *Last Letters of Aubrey Beardsley*, London, 1904. The other series appeared also in mutilated form, edited by R. A. Walker in *Letters from Aubrey Beardsley to Leonard Smithers*, London, 1937.

that imitators did so shows how little they understood the strength of his mind or the integrity of his best work. Today his record can be viewed with composure if we stand back from it to reflect that evaluations vary according to the age and position of each creature in its evolutionary group: that the morals and ideals of the Victorians were maintained at the expense of new life: that one monster's evil may be some other monster's good.

Illustrations

Reproductions of original drawings by Aubrey Beardsley, or of plates after drawings by him. Unless stated otherwise the drawings are in indian ink.

Cover: Panel from title-page of *The Dancing Faun* by Florence Farr (Keynotes Series), London, 1894. From line-block (enlarged).

Page 1 (headpiece): Vignette in *Bon-Mots of Sydney Smith and R. B. Sheridan*, London, 1893, p. 26. From the original drawing, reproduced by courtesy of R. A. Harari, Esq., London.

THE PLATES

1 (*top*) Initial A for Book II, Chapter I, in *Le Morte d'Arthur*, Vol. I, London, 1893. From the original drawing in the Victoria and Albert Museum.

1 (*bottom*) Heading for Book IV, Chapter X, etc., in *Le Morte d'Arthur*, Vol. I, London, 1893. From the original drawing in the Victoria and Albert Museum.

2 (*top*) Heading for Book VI, Chapter IX, etc., in *Le Morte d'Arthur*, Vol. I, London, 1893. From the original drawing, reproduced by courtesy of the Western Australian Art Gallery, Perth, Western Australia.

2 (*bottom*) Heading for Book XIII, Chapter XVII, in *Le Morte d'Arthur*, Vol. II, London, 1894. From the original drawing in the Victoria and Albert Museum.

3 How King Arthur saw the Questing Beast. Published in photogravure as frontispiece to *Le Morte d'Arthur*, Vol. I, London, 1893. From the original drawing, reproduced by courtesy of R. A. Harari, Esq., London.

4 Merlin and Nimue. Full-page illustration in *Le Morte d'Arthur*, Vol. I, London, 1893, facing p. 106. From line-block.

5 How Sir Tristram drank of the Love Drink. Full-page illustration in *Le Morte d'Arthur*, London, Vol. I, 1893, facing p. 334. From line-block.

6 (*top*) Vignette in *Bon-Mots of Sydney Smith and R. B. Sheridan*, London, 1893, p. 101. From the original drawing, reproduced by courtesy of R. A. Harari, Esq., London.

6 (*bottom*) Vignette in *Bon-Mots of Sydney Smith and R. B. Sheridan*, London, 1893, p. 109. From the original drawing, reproduced by courtesy of R. A. Harari, Esq., London.

7 (*top*) Vignette in *Bon-Mots of Sydney Smith and R. B. Sheridan*, London, 1893, p. 136. From the original drawing, reproduced by courtesy of R. A. Harari, Esq., London.

7 (*bottom*) Vignette in *Bon-Mots of Sydney Smith and R. B. Sheridan*, London, 1893, p. 150. From the original drawing in the Grenville L. Winthrop Gift, Fogg Art Museum. Reproduced by courtesy of Fogg Art Museum, Harvard University, Cambridge, Massachusetts, U.S.A.

8 (*top*) Vignette in *Bon-Mots of Sydney Smith and R. B. Sheridan*, London, 1893, p. 170. From the original drawing, reproduced by courtesy of R. A. Harari, Esq., London.

8 (*bottom*) Vignette in *Bon-Mots of Sydney Smith and R. B. Sheridan*, London, 1893, p. 186. From the original drawing, reproduced by courtesy of R. A. Harari, Esq., London.

9 (*top*) Vignette in *Bon Mots of Charles Lamb and Douglas Jerrold*, London, 1893, p. 75. From the original drawing, reproduced by courtesy of R. A. Harari, Esq., London.

9 (*bottom*) Vignette in *Bon-Mots of Charles Lamb and Douglas Jerrold*, London, 1893, p. 156. From the original drawing, reproduced by courtesy of R. A. Harari, Esq., London.

10 (*top*) Vignette in *Bon-Mots of Sammuel Foote and Theodore Hook*, London, 1894, p. 56. From line-block.

10 (*bottom*) Headpiece in *St. Paul's*, 20th July, 1895. The drawing dated from 1893. From line-block.

11 Débris d'un Poète. From the original drawing in the Victoria and Albert Museum.

12 Frontispiece to *The Wonderful History of Vergilius the Sorcerer*, London, 1893. From the original drawing, reproduced by courtesy of the Art Institute of Chicago, U.S.A.

13 Incipit Vita Nova. Reproduction in half-tone from half-tone plate.

14 The Kiss of Judas. Published in *The Pall Mall Magazine*, July, 1893. From the original drawing, reproduced by courtesy of R. A. Harari, Esq., London.

15 John and Salomé. Intended as one of the series illustrating *Salomé* by Oscar Wilde, translated by Lord Alfred Douglas, London, 1894. Not used, and first published in *The Early Work of Aubrey Beardsley*, London, 1899. From the original drawing in the Grenville L. Winthrop Bequest, Fogg Art Museum. Reproduced by courtesy of Fogg Art Museum, Harvard University, Cambridge, Massachusetts, U.S.A.

16 The Woman in the Moon. Frontispiece to *Salomé* by Oscar Wilde, translated by Lord Alfred Douglas, London, 1894. From the original drawing in the Grenville L. Winthrop Bequest, Fogg Art Museum. Reproduced by courtesy of Fogg Art Museum, Harvard University, Cambridge, Massachusetts, U.S.A.

17 The Peacock Skirt. Plate II in series illustrating *Salomé* by Oscar Wilde, translated by Lord Alfred Douglas, London, 1894. From the original drawing in the Grenville L. Winthrop Bequest, Fogg Art Museum. Reproduced by courtesy of Fogg Art Museum, Harvard University, Cambridge, Massachusetts, U.S.A.

18 The Toilet of Salomé. Plate VIII (substituted for withdrawn design) in series illustrating *Salomé* by Oscar Wilde, translated by Lord Alfred Douglas, London, 1894. From the original drawing, reproduced by courtesy of the Trustees of the British Museum.

19 Frontispiece to *Plays by John Davidson*, London, 1894; with caricatures (from left) of Mabel Beardsley, Henry Harland, Oscar Wilde, Sir Augustus Harris, Richard Le Gallienne and Adeline Genée. From the original drawing, reproduced by courtesy of the Trustees of the Tate Gallery.

20 L'Éducation Sentimentale. Illustration of theme of Flaubert's work of that name: published in *The Yellow Book*, Vol. I, April, 1894. From left half only of the original drawing (later divided) in the Grenville L. Winthrop Bequest, Fogg Art Museum. Reproduced by courtesy of Fogg Art Museum, Harvard University, Cambridge, Massachusetts, U.S.A.

21 Night Piece. Published (half-tone) in *The Yellow Book*, Vol. I, April, 1894. From the original drawing, reproduced by permission of the Syndics of the Fitzwilliam Museum, Cambridge, England.

22 The Fat Woman (a caricature of Mrs Whistler). Published in *To-Day*, 12th May, 1894. From the original drawing, reproduced by courtesy of the Trustees of the Tate Gallery.

23 Comedy-Ballet of Marionettes, II. Published in *The Yellow Book*, Vol. II, July, 1894. From line-block.

24 Garçons de Café. Published in *The Yellow Book*, Vol. II, July, 1894. From line-block.

25 Cover of *The Yellow Book*, Vol. III, October, 1894. From line-block.

26 La Dame aux Camélias. Illustration of theme of the work of that name by Dumas *fils*, published in *The Yellow Book*, Vol. III, October, 1894. From the original drawing, reproduced by courtesy of the Trustees of the Tate Gallery.

27 Lady Gold's Escort. Published in *The Yellow Book*, Vol. III, October, 1894. From line-block.

28 The Wagnerites. Published in *The Yellow Book*, Vol. III, October, 1894. From the original drawing in the Victoria and Albert Museum.

29 Invitation card for the opening of the Prince's Ladies Golf Club, Mitcham, 1894. From line-block.

30 The Mysterious Rose Garden. Published in *The Yellow Book*, Vol. IV, January, 1895. From the original drawing in the Grenville L. Winthrop Bequest, Fogg Art Museum. Reproduced by courtesy of Fogg Art Museum, Harvard University, Cambridge, Massachusetts, U.S.A.

31 Frontispiece to *The Wonderful Mission of Earl Lavender* by John Davidson, London, 1895. From the original drawing in the Grenville L. Winthrop Bequest, Fogg Art Museum. Reproduced by courtesy of Fogg Art Museum, Harvard University, Cambridge, Massachusetts, U.S.A.

32 Atalanta. Intended for publication in *The Yellow Book*, Vol. V, April, 1895. From the original drawing, reproduced by courtesy of the Trustees of the British Museum.

33 Design for the cover of *The Savoy*, No. 1, January, 1896. From the original drawing in the Grenville L. Winthrop Bequest, Fogg Art Museum. Reproduced by courtesy of Fogg Art Museum, Harvard University, Cambridge, Massachusetts, U.S.A.

34 The Abbé. Illustration to *Under the Hill* by Aubrey Beardsley, published in

The Savoy, No. 1, January, 1896. From the original drawing, reproduced by courtesy of R. A. Harari, Esq., London.

35 The Return of Tannhäuser to Venusberg. Originally intended as illustration to *Under the Hill* by Aubrey Beardsley. From line-block.

36 Lysistrata haranguing the Athenian Women. The third of eight illustrations to *The Lysistrata of Aristophanes*, London, 1896. From the original drawing, reproduced by courtesy of R. A. Harari, Esq., London.

37 Design for the cover of *The Rape of the Lock* (Alexander Pope), London, 1896. From the original drawing, reproduced by courtesy of R. A. Harari, Esq., London.

38 The Battle of the Beaux and the Belles. Plate VIII in *The Rape of the Lock* (Alexander Pope), London, 1896. From the original drawing, reproduced by permission of the Barber Institute of Fine Arts, University of Birmingham.

39 The Coiffing. Illustration to *The Ballad of a Barber* by Aubrey Beardsley, published in *The Savoy*, No. 3, July, 1896. From line-block.

40 The Fourth Tableau of "Das Rheingold". Design for the cover of *The Savoy* No. 6, October, 1896. From the original drawing, reproduced by courtesy of R. A. Harari, Esq., London.

41 Frontispiece to *The Pierrot of the Minute* by Ernest Dowson, London, 1897. From line-block.

42 Messalina returning from the Bath. Intended for illustration to the *Sixth Satire* of Juvenal. From the original drawing, reproduced by courtesy of R. A. Harari, Esq., London.

43 Aubrey Beardsley's bookplate (used by Herbert J. Pollitt). From line-block.

44 Ali Baba. Cover design intended for *The Forty Thieves*. From the original drawing in the Grenville L. Winthrop Bequest, Fogg Art Museum. Reproduced by courtesy of Fogg Art Museum, Harvard University, Cambridge, Massachusetts, U.S.A.

45 Design for the cover of *The Houses of Sin* by Vincent O'Sullivan, London, 1897. From line-block.

46 The Lady at the Dressing Table. No. IV of six illustrations to *Mademoiselle de Maupin* by Théophile Gautier, published in portfolio by Leonard Smithers, London, 1898. From photogravure.

47 The Lady with the Monkey. No. VI of six illustrations to *Mademoiselle de Maupin* by Théophile Gautier, published in portfolio by Leonard Smithers, London, 1898. From the original indian ink and wash drawing, reproduced by courtesy of R. A. Harari, Esq., London.

48 Frontispiece to *Volpone, or the Foxe* (Ben Jonson), London, 1898. From line-block.

49 Initial S published in *Volpone, or the Foxe* (Ben Jonson), London, 1898. From the original drawing in pen and crayon in the Grenville L. Winthrop Bequest, Fogg Art Museum. Reproduced by courtesy of Fogg Art Museum, Harvard University, Cambridge, Massachusetts, U.S.A.

50 Sketch of a child, in pencil and pen. From half-tone plate.

MERLIN AND NIMVE

HOW SIR TRISTRAM
DRANK OF THE
LOVE DRINK

5

6

8

9

10

LE DÈBRIS
D'VN POÈTE.

12

13

THE · KISS · OF
JVDAS

14

19

20

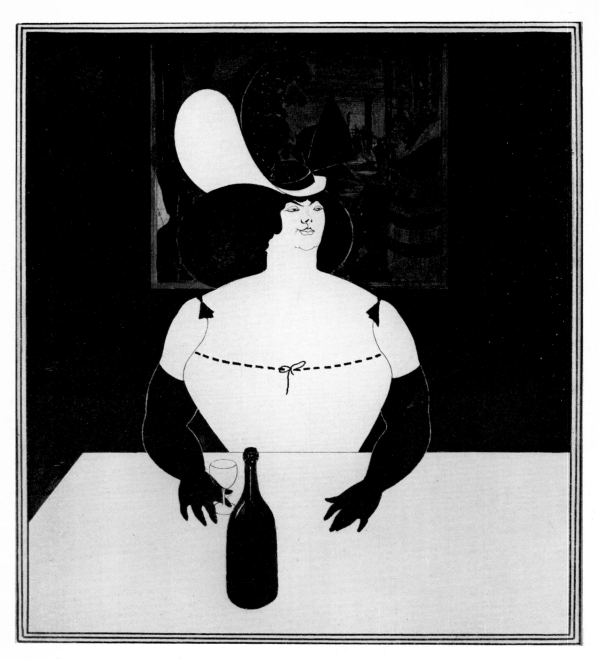

22

24

The Yellow Book

An Illustrated Quarterly

Volume III October 1894

Price $1.50 Net

London: John Lane
Boston: Copeland & Day

Price 5/- Net

26

27

28

AVBREY
BEARDSLEY

AUBREY
BEARDSLEY

34

35

AVBREY BEARDSLEY.

36

38

AUBREY BEARDSLEY.

39

MESSALINA.

43

44

45

46

47

48

49

50